# Carols from Around the World

**Nine Carols from the UK, USA, Germany, France and Spain Arranged for Piano Solo**

Darrell Archer

WWW.MELBAY.COM

# Preface

I have long wanted to develop a book featuring many well-known Christmas carols derived from a variety of countries and cultures. Hopefully this collection will acquaint pianists and listeners alike with some of these songs and their sources. It is my sincere desire that this book will bring new life and familiarity to these lovely works. It is with this idea in mind that I enthusiastically present this collection of carols and holiday songs for your enjoyment.

# Table of Contents

# Auld Lang Syne

Traditional Scottish Melody
Arr. Darrell V. Archer

17
F△9 F Dm9 Dm7 Gm Gm7 Gm6/A A7 Dm Gm7 C7 F
dim.
mp
poco a poco rit. a cresc.

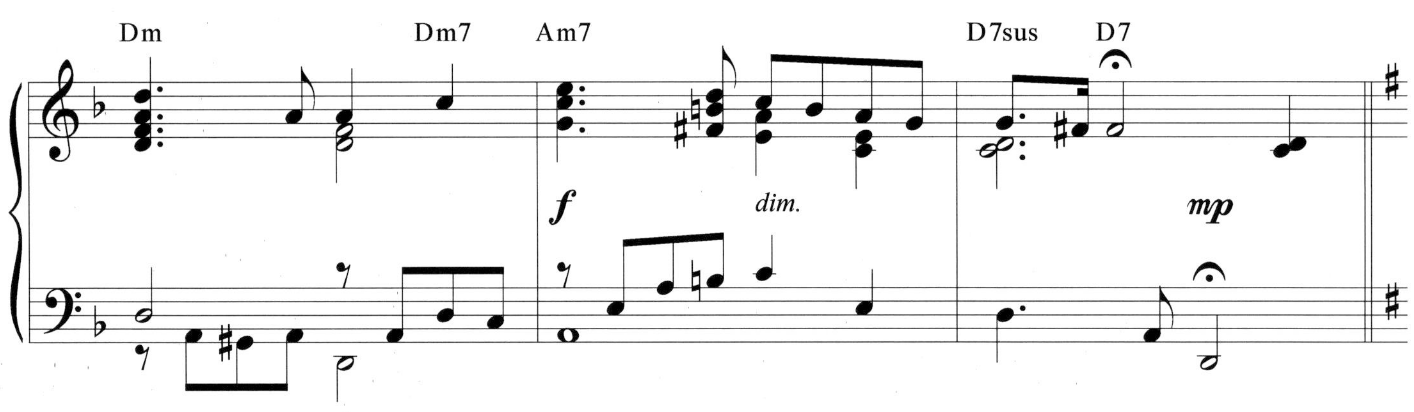
Dm Dm7 Am7 D7sus D7
f
dim.
mp

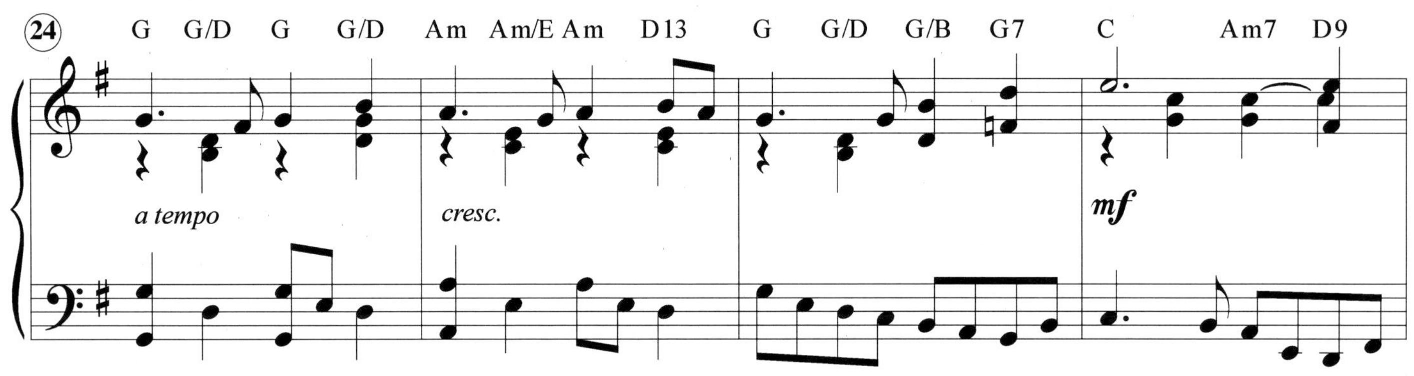
24
G G/D G G/D Am Am/E Am D13 G G/D G/B G7 C Am7 D9
a tempo
cresc.
mf

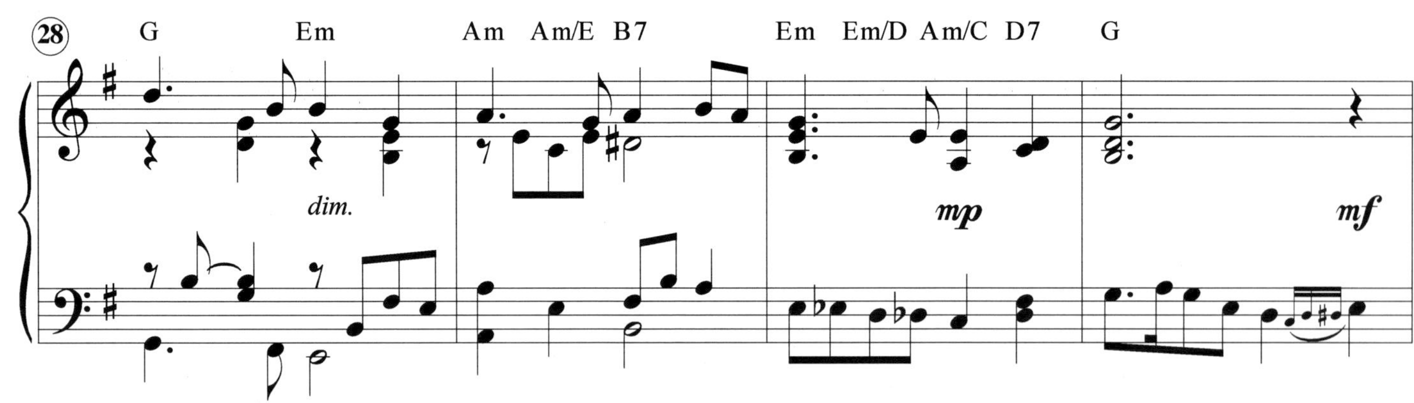
28
G Em Am Am/E B7 Em Em/D Am/C D7 G
dim.
mp
mf

32
Rhythm Tacet
mp
Broader
3
3
3
cresc. e rit.
f

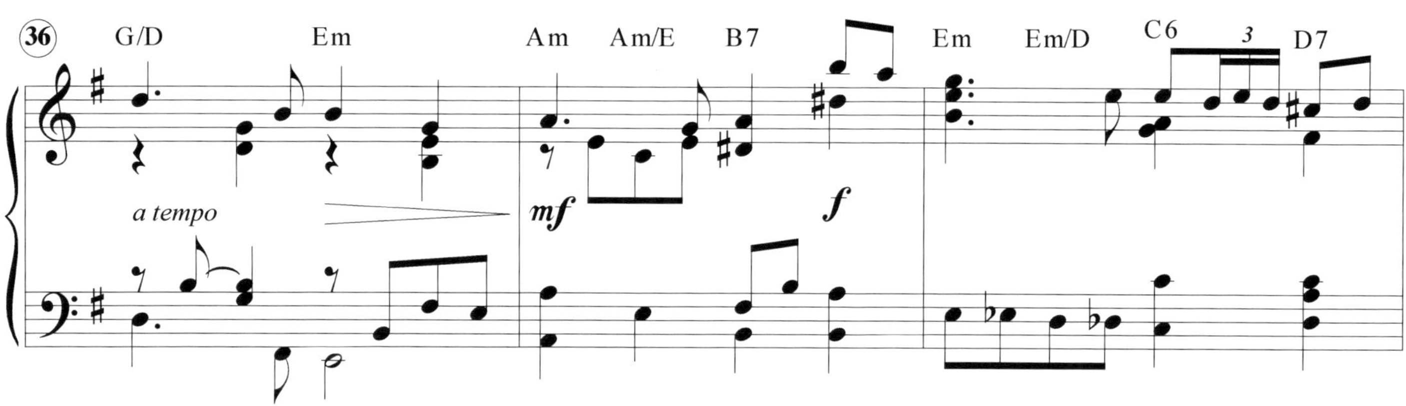
36
G/D
Em
Am
Am/E
B7
Em
Em/D
C6
3
D7
a tempo
mf
f

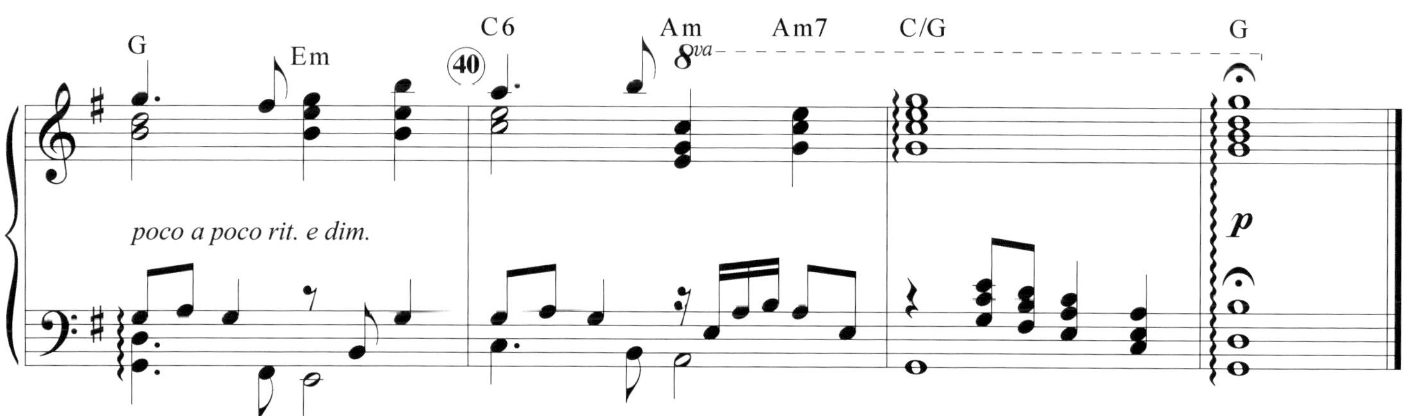
G
Em
C6
40
Am
8va
Am7
C/G
G
poco a poco rit. e dim.
p

# Bring a Torch, Jeanette Isabella

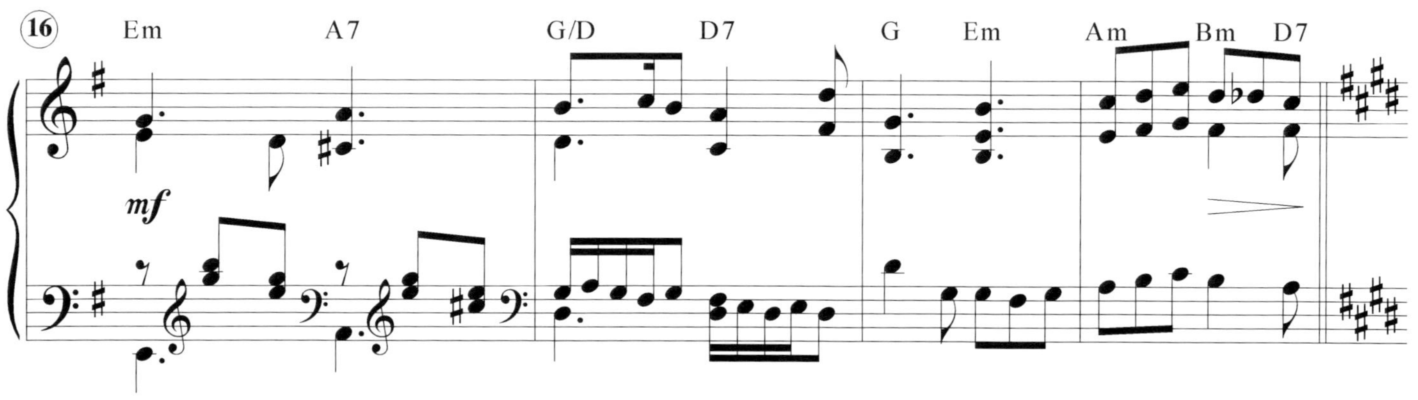
16
Em
A7
G/D
D7
G
Em
Am
Bm
D7
mf

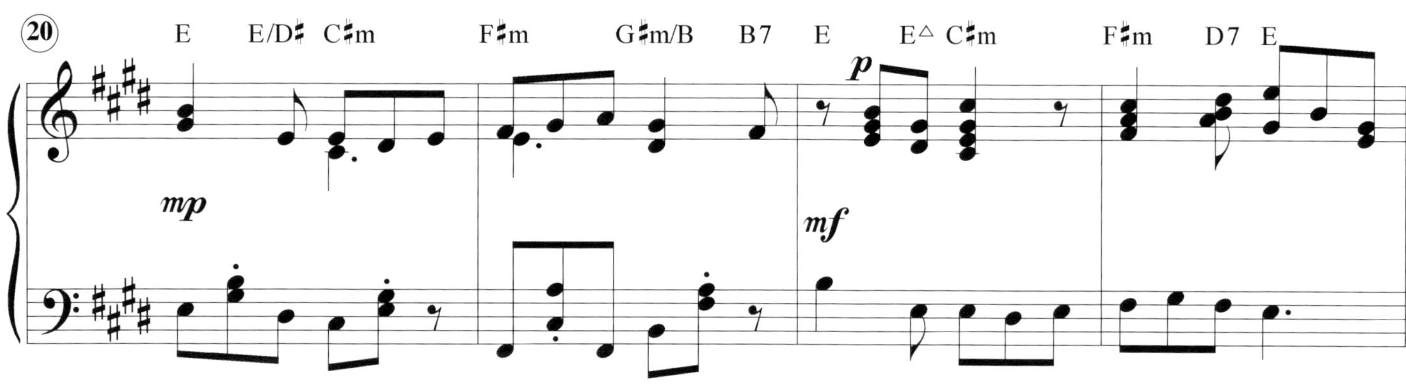
20
E
E/D♯
C♯m
F♯m
G♯m/B
B7
E
E△
C♯m
F♯m
D7
E
mp
p
mf

24
E/D♯
C♯m
F♯m7
F♯m7/B
B7
A
E
F♯m
B
B7
mp
f

28
Rhythm Tacet
31
C♯m
F♯
p
mf
f

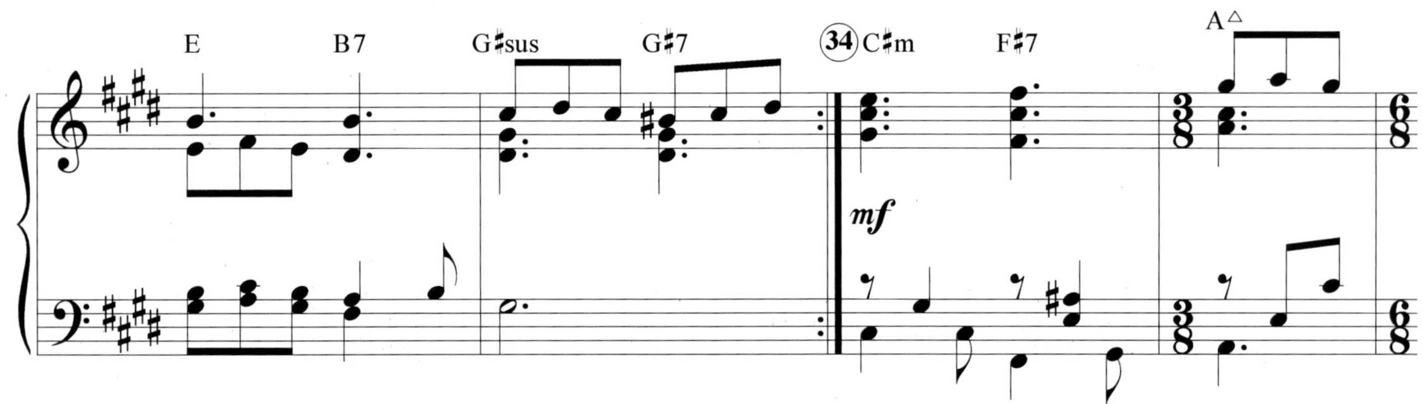
E
B7
G♯sus
G♯7
34
C♯m
F♯7
A△
mf

B
B7/D♯
B7
C♯
C♯/B♯
A♯m
A♯m/E♯
D♯m
Fm/G♯
A♭7/C
f

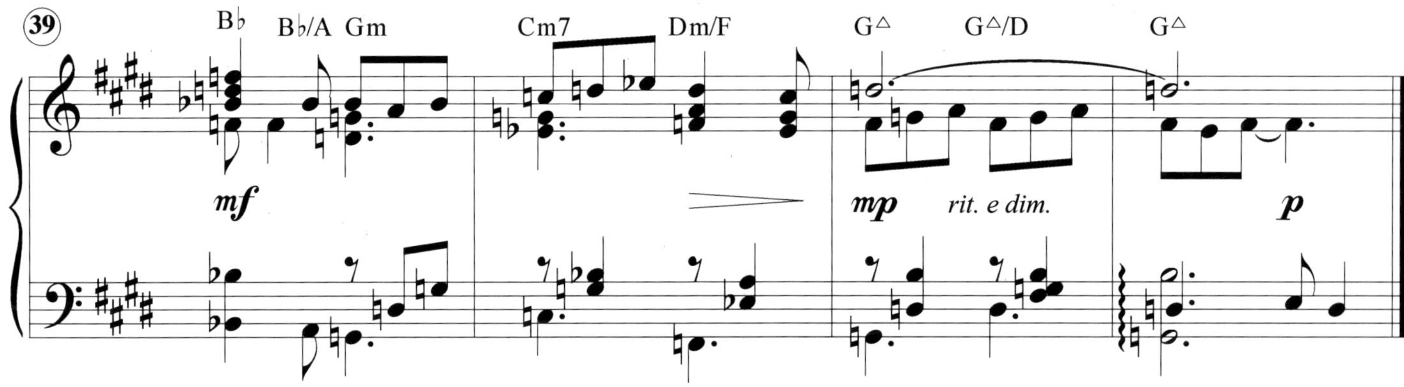
39
B♭
B♭/A
Gm
Cm7
Dm/F
G△
G△/D
G△
mf
mp
rit. e dim.
p

# Christ Was Born on Christmas Day

14th Century German Tune
Arr. Darrell V. Archer

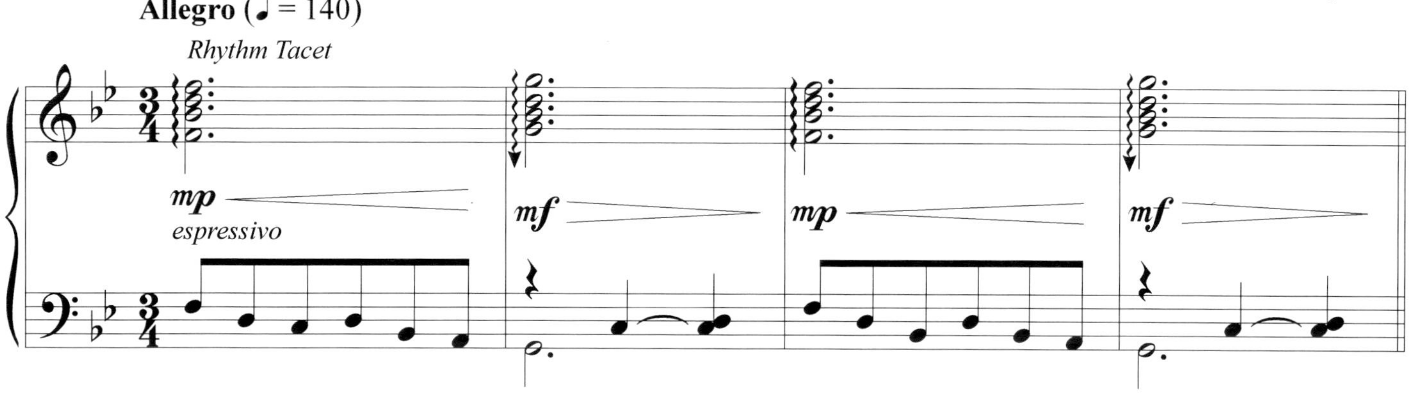


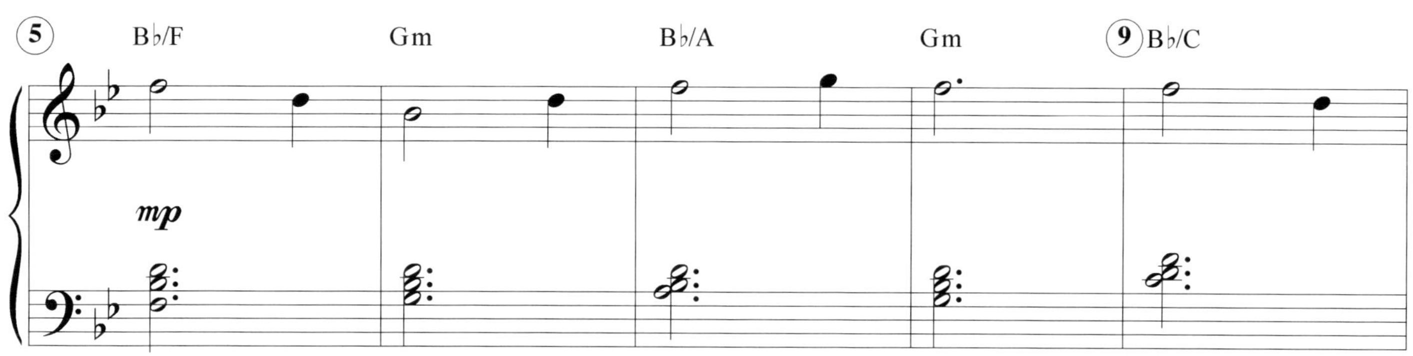


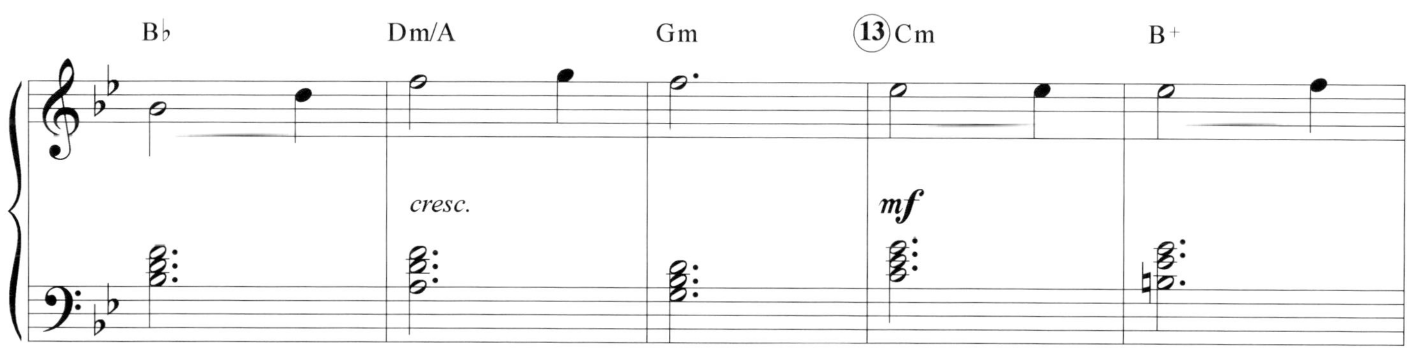


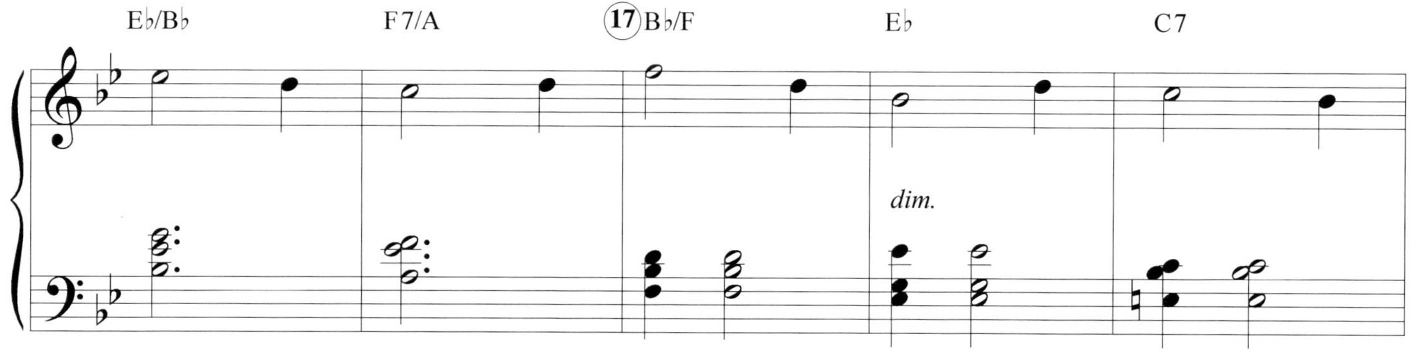

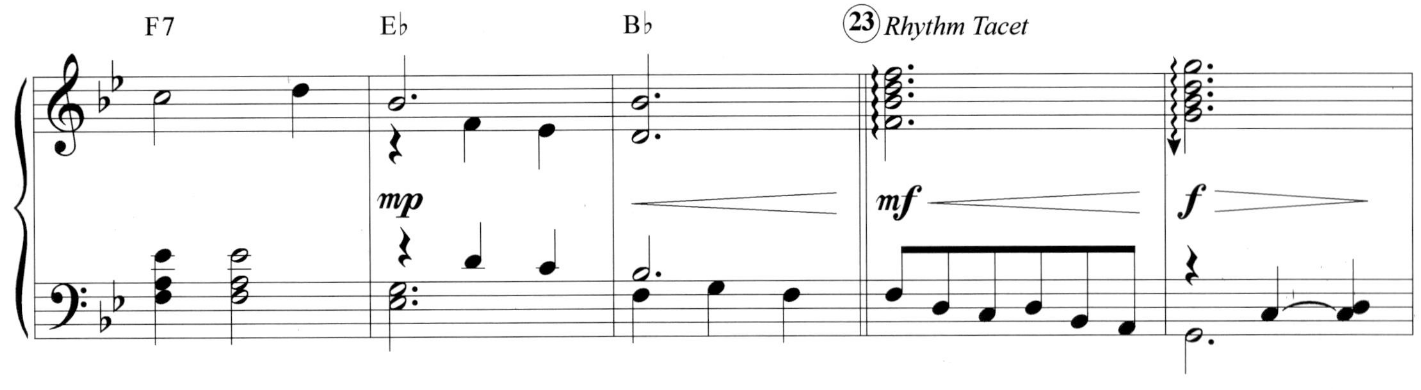
F7
E♭
B♭
23 Rhythm Tacet
mp
mf
f

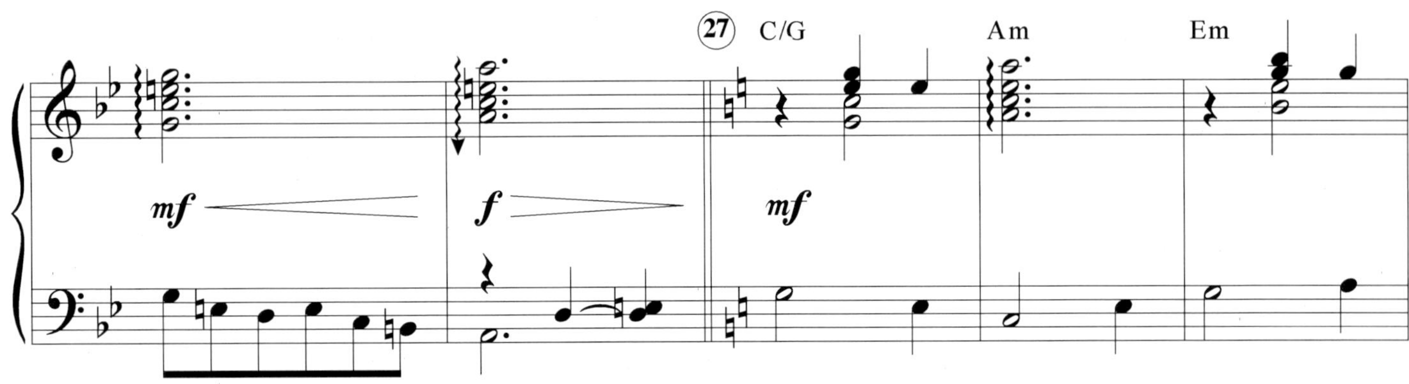
27 C/G
Am
Em
mf
f
mf

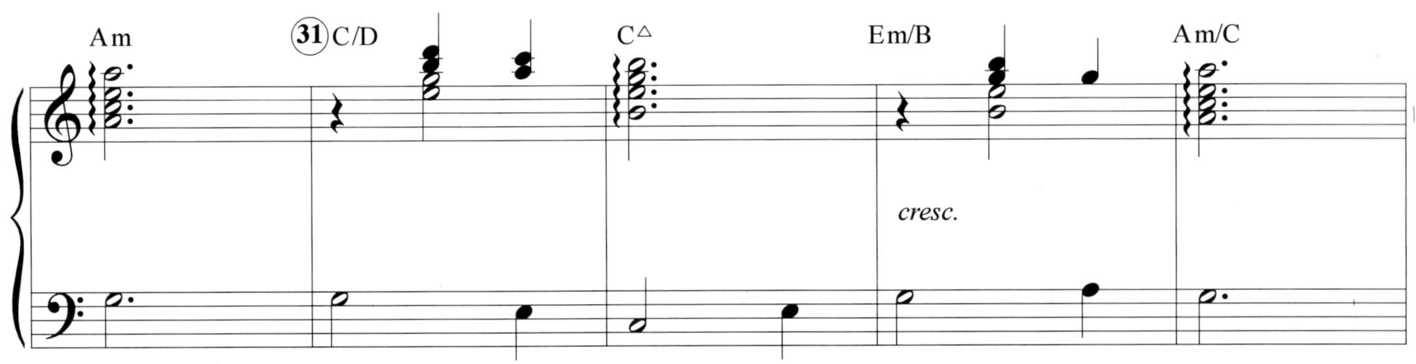
Am
31 C/D
C△
Em/B
Am/C
cresc.

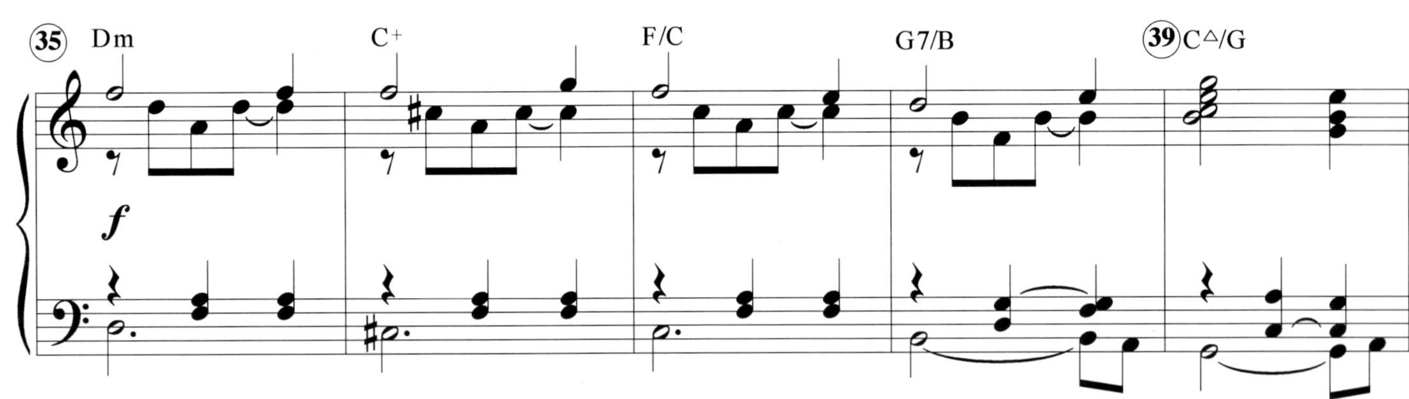
35 Dm
C+
F/C
G7/B
39 C△/G
f

F△
D 9/6
G9
Em/G
F 9/6
C 9/6
dim.
mf
45
Em
D♯+
G/D
A7/C♯
49
D△/A
f
G△
E 9/6
A9
F♯m/A
53
G 9/6
dim.
mf
D 9/6
mp
mf
molto rit. e dim.
p

# That Beautiful Name

Mabel Johnston Camp
Arr. Darrell V. Archer

Jean Perry, alt.

17
3
mf
mp

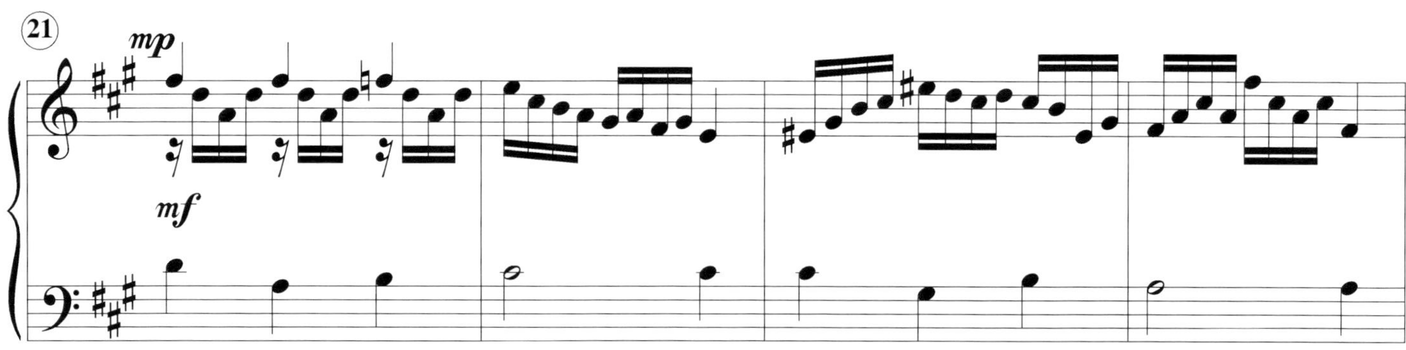
21
mp
mf

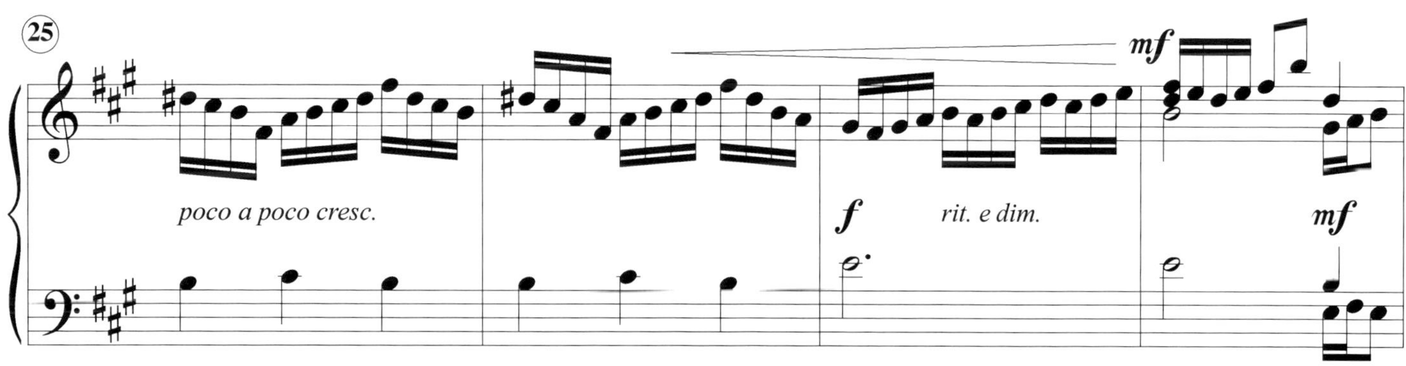
25
mf
poco a poco cresc.
f
rit. e dim.
mf

29
a tempo
poco a poco rit. e cresc.
f
mf

33
a tempo
3
rit. e dim.
mp

37
più mosso

41
8va
p

45
(8va)

49
poco a poco rit. e cresc.
a tempo
mp
mf
mel.
53
mp
mp
A sus
60
3
3
rit. e cresc.
3
mf
f
Broader

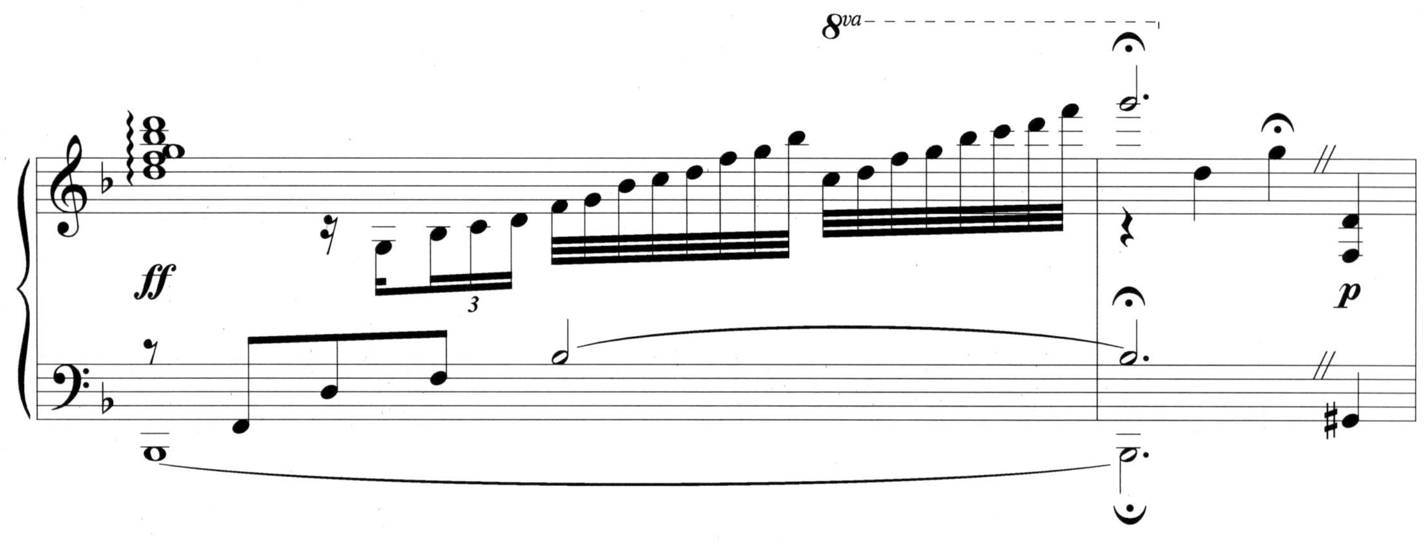
8va
ff
p

66
3
poco a poco rit. e cresc.
a tempo
molto dim.
3

p
3
mp
3
poco a poco rit. e dim.
R.H.
3
8va
pp

# Child in the Manger

Mary MacDonald
Trans. by Lochlan MacBean

Traditional Gaelic Melody
Arr. Darrell V. Archer

C△
F
G7
1. Csus
C
mf
mp
2.
C
C7
F
3
12
F
Gm
C7
3
cresc.
mf
B♭
F
Dm
Am
B♭
F△/A
E♭
C7
F
16
Dm
B♭
F
mp
dim.
p
molto rit. e cresc.
f
Broadly

Dm
G
C13
F
B♭
C7
mp
mf a tempo
(♭)

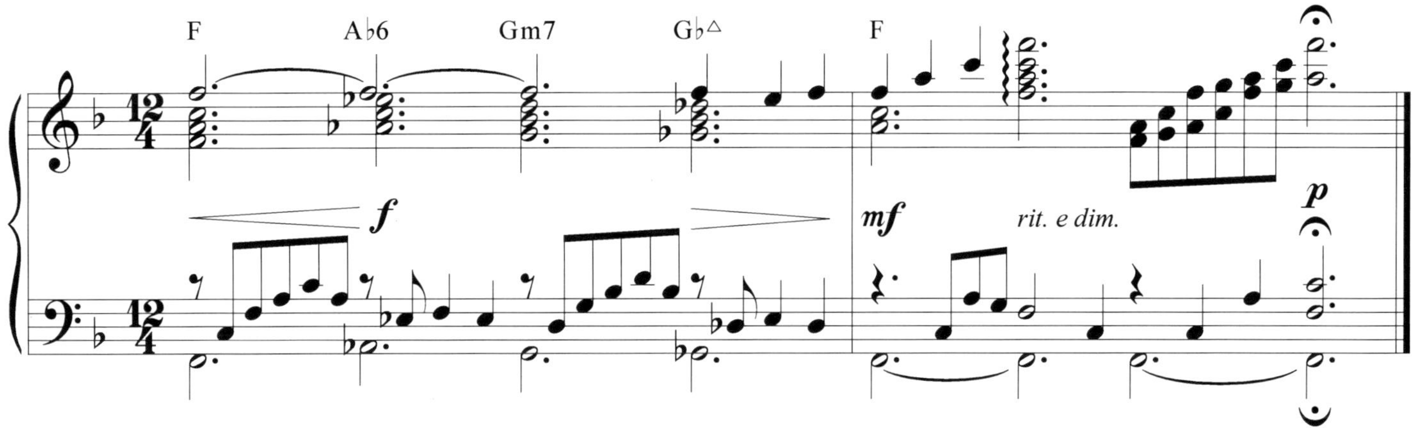
F
A♭6
Gm7
G♭△
F
f
mf
rit. e dim.
p

# Infant Holy, Infant Lowly

Para. by Edith M. G. Reed

Polish Carol
Arr. Darrell V. Archer

17
G/B
C6
D13
D♯°7
Em
Bm/D
C
G/B
C
D13
D9
G
Rhythm Tacet
f
mf
p
mp
21
mf
mp
25
mf
8va
E+
29
F
Dm
G
G7
E
Am
F
Fm/A♭
poco a poco cresc.

G
Rhythm Tacet
33
f
mp
p
poco a poco rit. e cresc.
f
mf
f
38
mf
p
mp
A
D/A
A
D6
E△
Broader
rit. e dim.
p

# Go Tell It on the Mountain

Arr. Darrell V. Archer

American Negro Spiritual
Compiled by John Wesley Work, Jr.

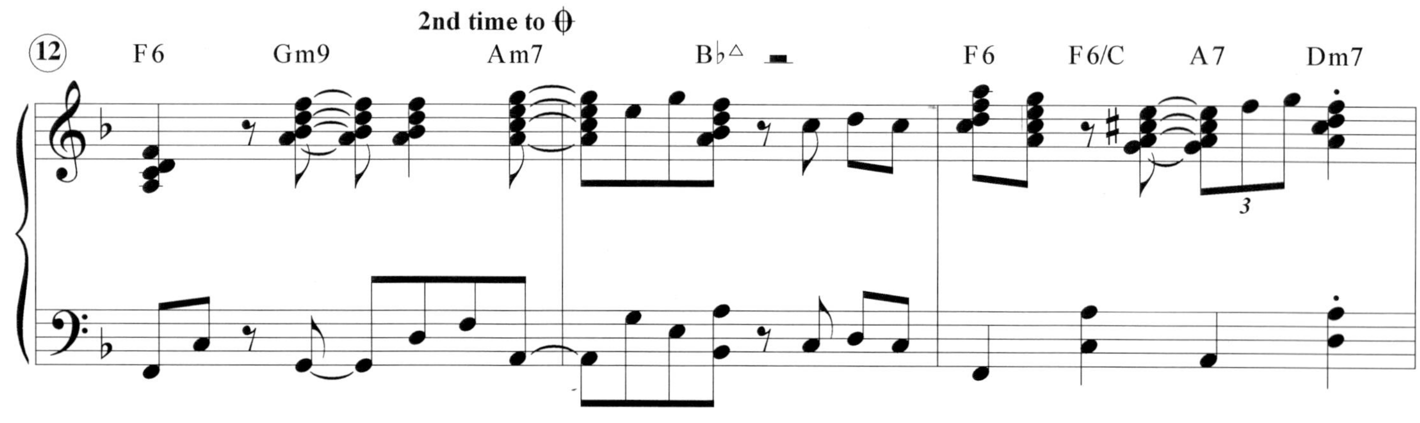
12
2nd time to ϕ
F6
Gm9
Am7
B♭△
F6
F6/C
A7
Dm7
3

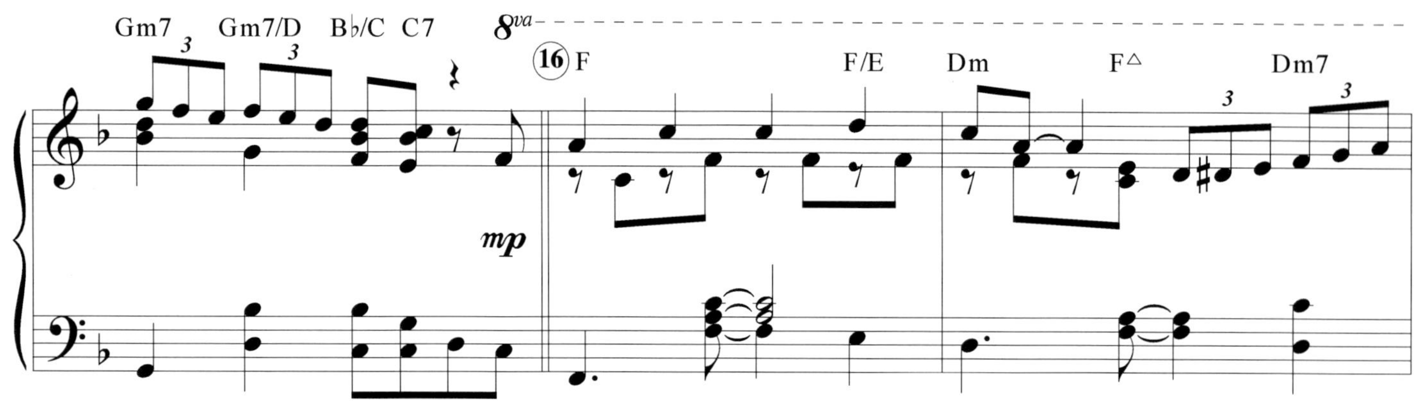
Gm7
Gm7/D
B♭/C
C7
8va
16
F
F/E
Dm
F△
Dm7
3
mp

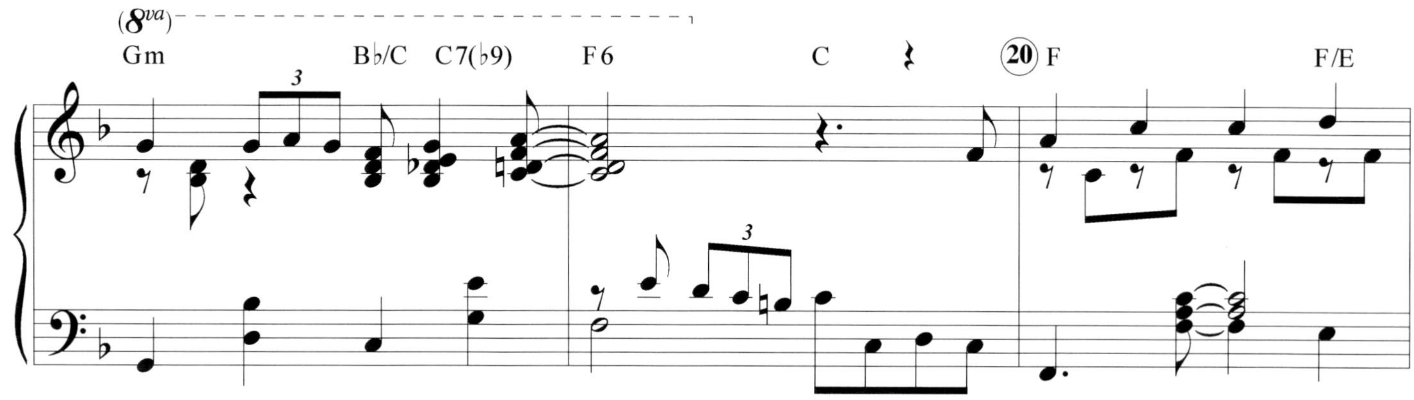
(8va)
Gm
B♭/C
C7(♭9)
F6
C
20
F
F/E
3

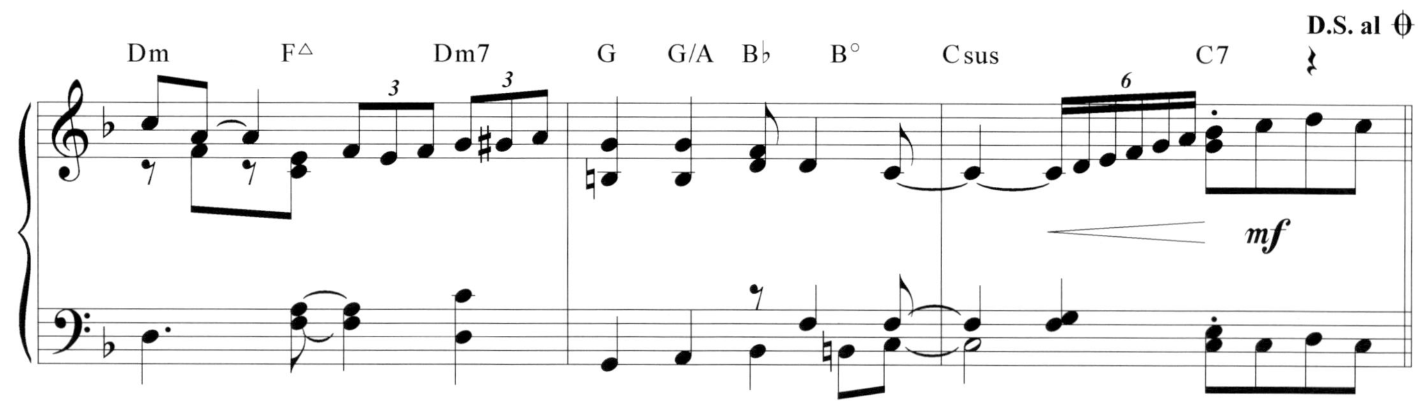
D.S. al ϕ
Dm
F△
Dm7
G
G/A
B♭
B°
Csus
C7
3
6
mf

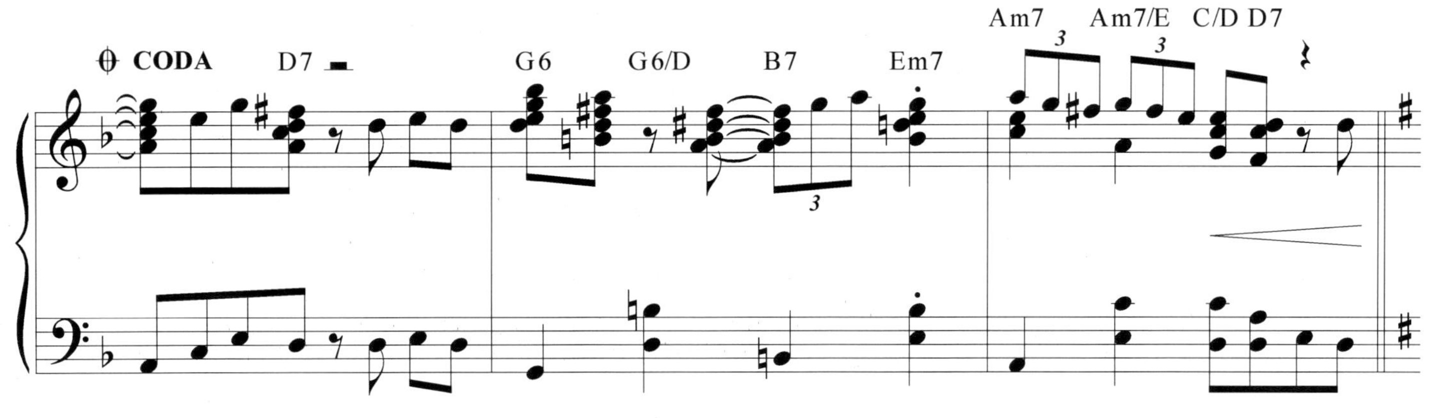
CODA
D7
G6
G6/D
B7
Em7
Am7
Am7/E
C/D D7
3

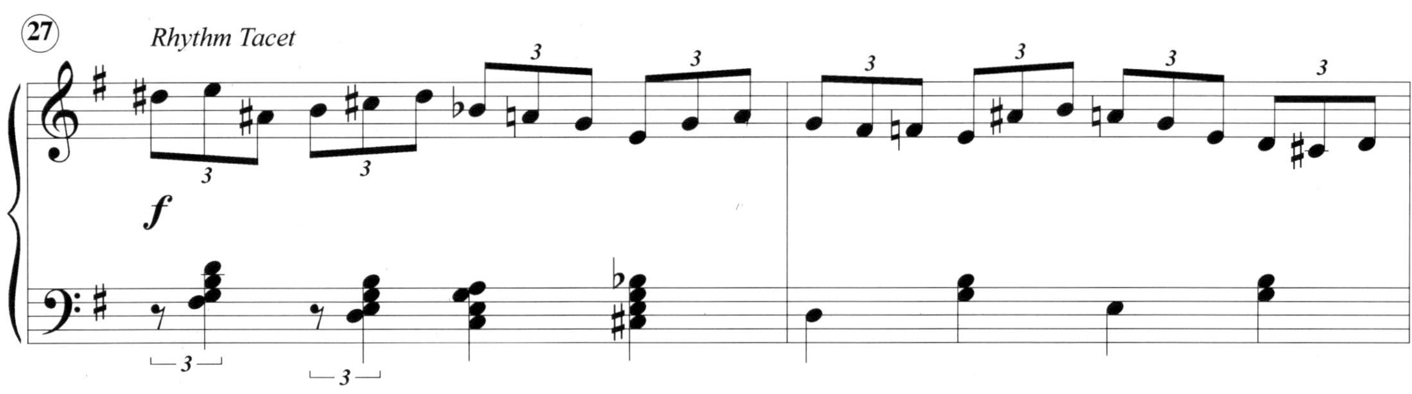
27
Rhythm Tacet
f
3

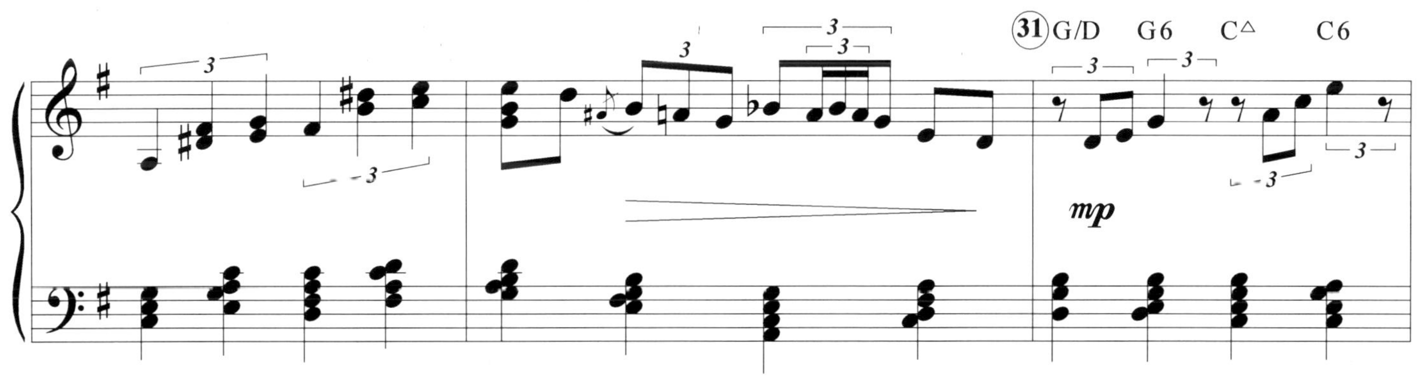
31
G/D
G6
C△
C6
mp
3

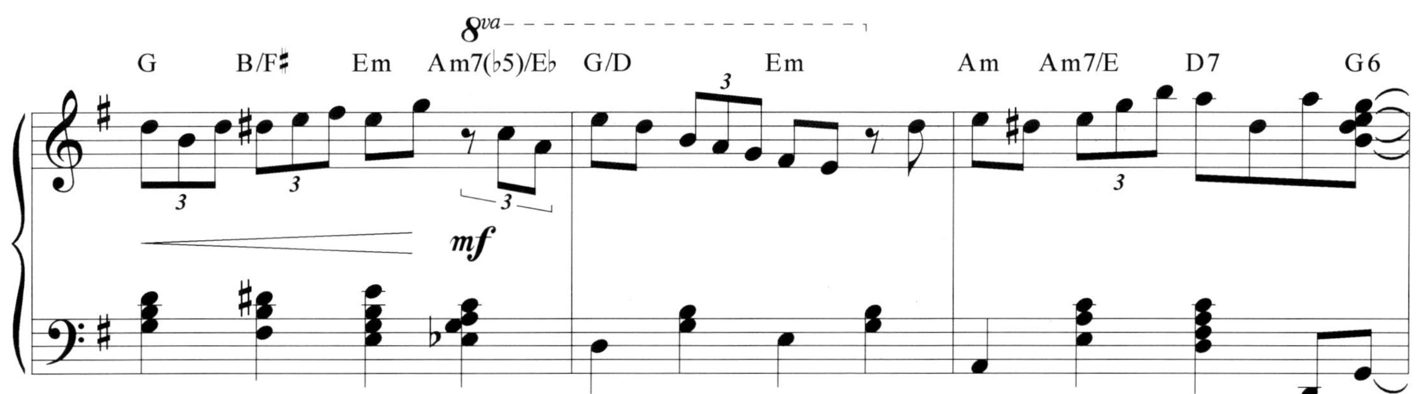
8va
G
B/F♯
Em
Am7(♭5)/E♭
G/D
Em
Am
Am7/E
D7
G6
mf
3

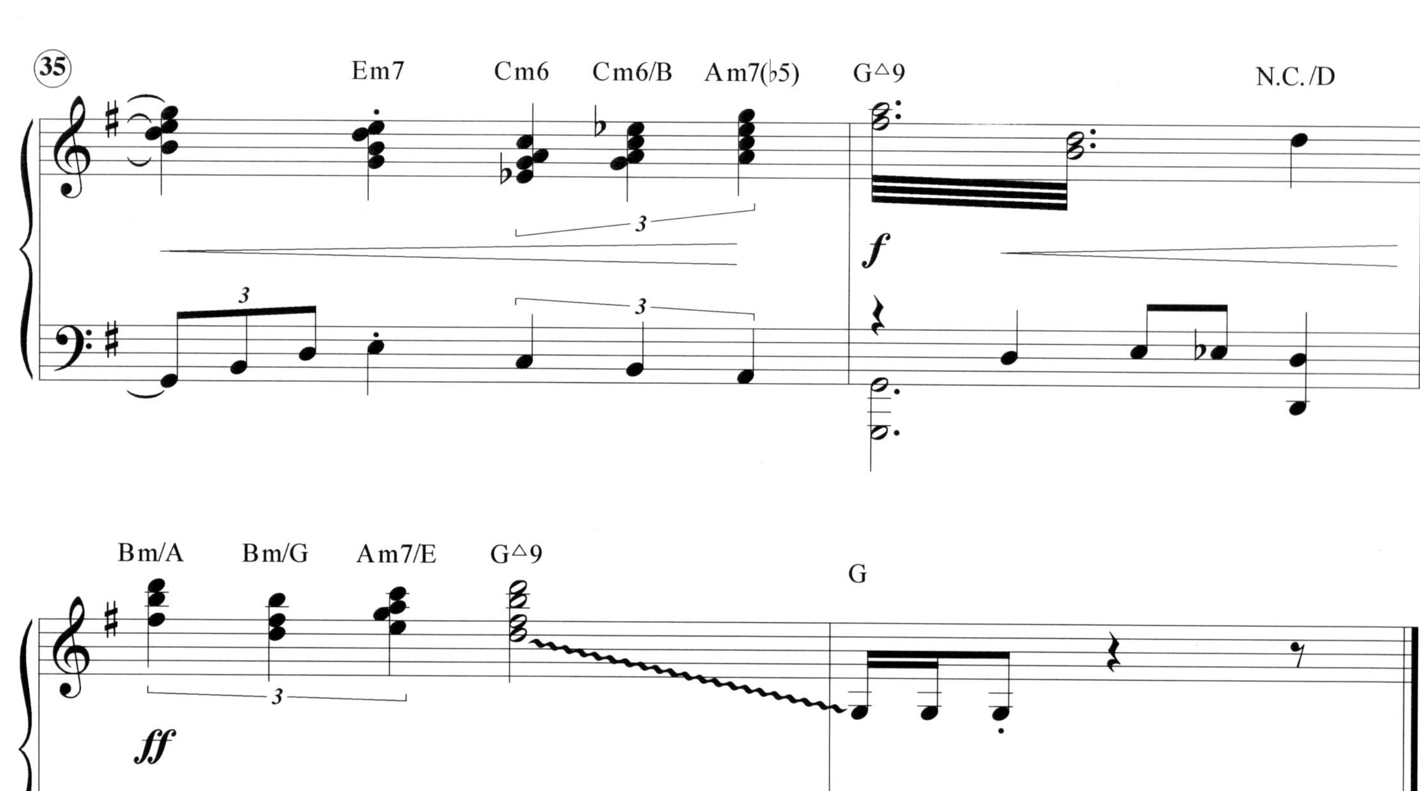
35
Em7
Cm6
Cm6/B
Am7(♭5)
G△9
N.C./D
3
f
Bm/A
Bm/G
Am7/E
G△9
G
ff

# Winds Through the Olive Trees

Traditional Carol from Gascony
Arr. Darrell V. Archer

Katherine Parker

mf
mp
mf
poco rit. e dim.
mp
cresc. e accel.
mf
molto rit.
C
L.H.
p
F
G
C
mf
R.H.
L.H.
A7
R.H.
D/F♯
D
D7/A
G7
C
C7
f
mf

8va
F
C/F
F♯+
Gm
C7
B♭
C7
12
8
p
poco cresc.
(8va)
F
D7
D+
D7
G
G7
mp
mf
(8va)
C7
B♭
C7
F
Rhythm Tacet
3
4
mp
mf
8va
C7
Gm7
C+
F
poco a poco rit. e dim.
mp
p

# Fum, Fum, Fum

16th Century Catalan Carol
Arr. Darrell V. Archer

Am E7 Am
14
E Am
Am6
mf

Am Dm E7 Am
Dm
E
18
Am
E7
p
mf

Am E7 Am
Am/E Am Am/E
Am
E7
Am G

22
C7/B♭ A♭°7 C(♭7)/G♭ Fm6
C7 D♭9
C D♭△ C
Rhythm Tacet
p
poco a

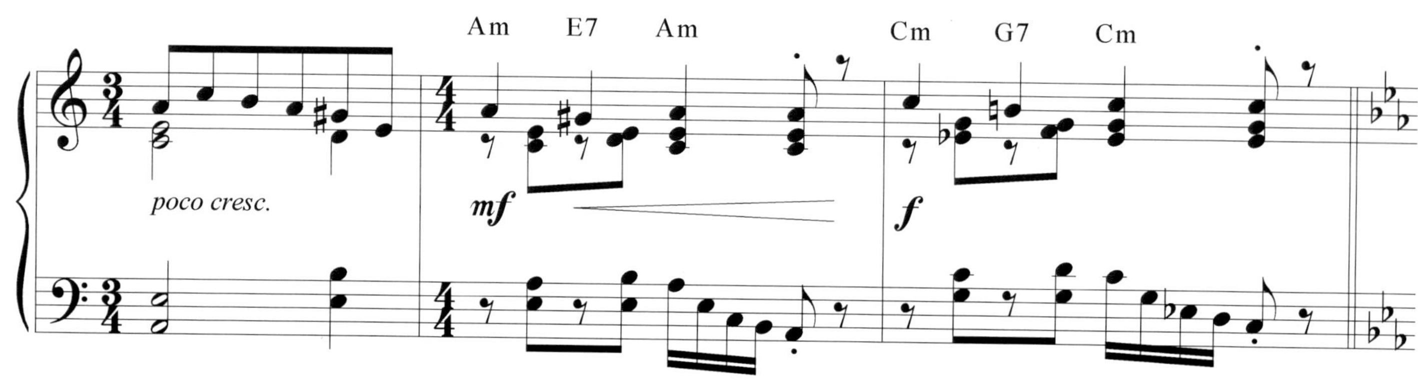
Am
E7
Am
Cm
G7
Cm
poco cresc.
mf
f

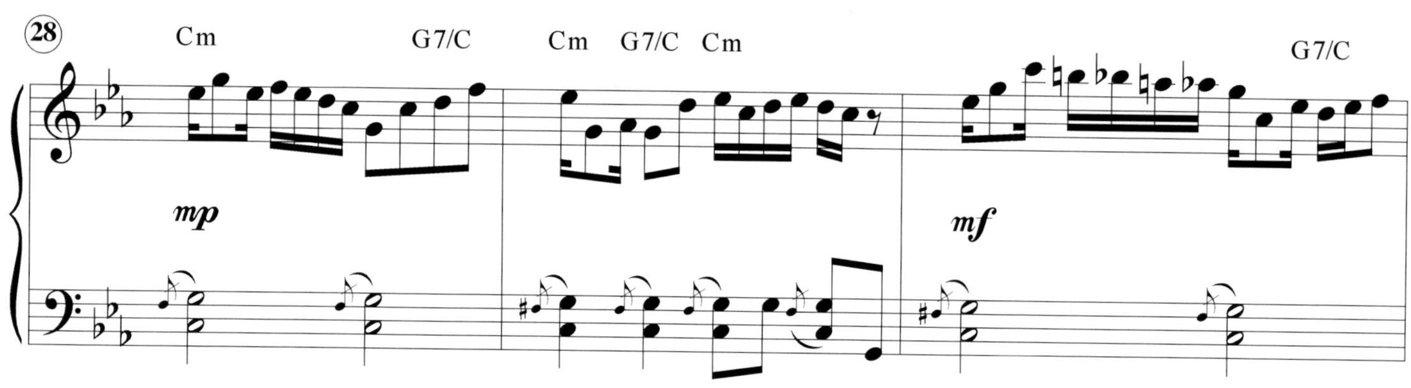
28
Cm
G7/C
Cm
G7/C
Cm
G7/C
mp
mf

Cm
G7/C
Cm
B♭
32
E♭
B♭
E♭
B♭7
E♭
B♭7
E
p

Rhythm Tacet
Cm
G7
Cm
poco a poco cresc.
mf

Dm
A7
Dm
38
A7
rit. e cresc.
f
Broader
Dm
A7
Dm
Dm6
Dm
A7
8va
8va
8va
Dm
A7
C
42
F
C7/G
F
C7
F
C7/G
F
8va
Gm
A7
Dm
dim. e rit.
mf
molto rit. e dim.

A7
mp
p
8va
48 Rhythm Tacet
3
f
ff
tr.
Dm
Em6
Dm
8va
Dm6
8va

# Other Mel Bay Sacred Piano Books

10 Gospel Favorites for Piano Solo (Archer)

12 Spirituals for Piano Solo (Gail Smith)

A Classic Christmas for Piano (Gail Smith)

Christian Classics for Piano Solo (Gail Smith)

Christmas Carols for Easy Piano (Benedict)

Christmas Carols for Piano Made Easy (Gail Smith)

Classical Piano for Worship Settings (Gail Smith)

Complete Church Pianist (Gail Smith)

Country Gospel Piano Solos (Gail Smith)

Easy Piano Solos for Worship (Shirley)

Easy Way Christmas Song Folio/Piano (S. Banks)

English Carols for Piano Solo (Gail Smith)

Favorite Hymns for Piano Solo (T. Price)

Favorite Hymns to Play for Piano (Leytham)

Gospel Piano Made Easy (Gail Smith)

Hymns Made Easy for Piano Book 1 (Gail Smith)

Hymns Made Easy for Piano Book 2 (Gail Smith)

Hymns Made Easy for Piano Book 3 (Gail Smith)

If Snowmen Could Make Music (Benedict)

Music Is for Everyone Christmas Book Level 1: For Young Children (Gilbert)

Old-Time Gospel Piano (Cummings/Whitmire)

Praise Piano Made Easy (Gail Smith)

Preludes and Offertories for Piano Solo (Gail Smith)

Wedding Music for Piano (T. Price)

WWW.MELBAY.COM